Spot the Magnets

Written by
Cath Jones

This is a magnet. Magnets do not all look the same. They can be big or little. They can be all sorts of shapes too.

Some people think that magnets attract all metals. But magnets are not attracted to things made of copper, silver or tin.

There are magnets inside lots of things, but we can't see them. They are hidden.

Lots of homes are filled with hidden magnets. Let's go on a magnet hunt to look for them.

Do you think you will spot some of these hidden magnets?

Are there magnets in this room? Yes! In fact, there might be lots.

How will this food stay cool? Magnets! A magnetic strip on the inside keeps it shut and helps keep the food cool.

How do these things stay out of the way? Magnets!

Magnets attract things made of steel.

These letters have magnets in them, so they stick to the steel.

Little magnets are good for sticking up notes too.

Do you have a cat?

If you do, you might have a cat flap. Can you spot the hidden magnets in the cat flap?

The cat flap clicks shut with a magnet. This helps keep the rain out and the heat in.

Lots of people have phones.

Can you spot the magnet in the phone case?

The magnet helps keep the case shut.

Lots of toys have magnets in them. Some of the toys have hidden magnets, but some magnets are not hidden.

The magnets stick things together. They act just like glue!

This toy has magnets to connect the parts.

This toy train is connected to the trucks with magnets.

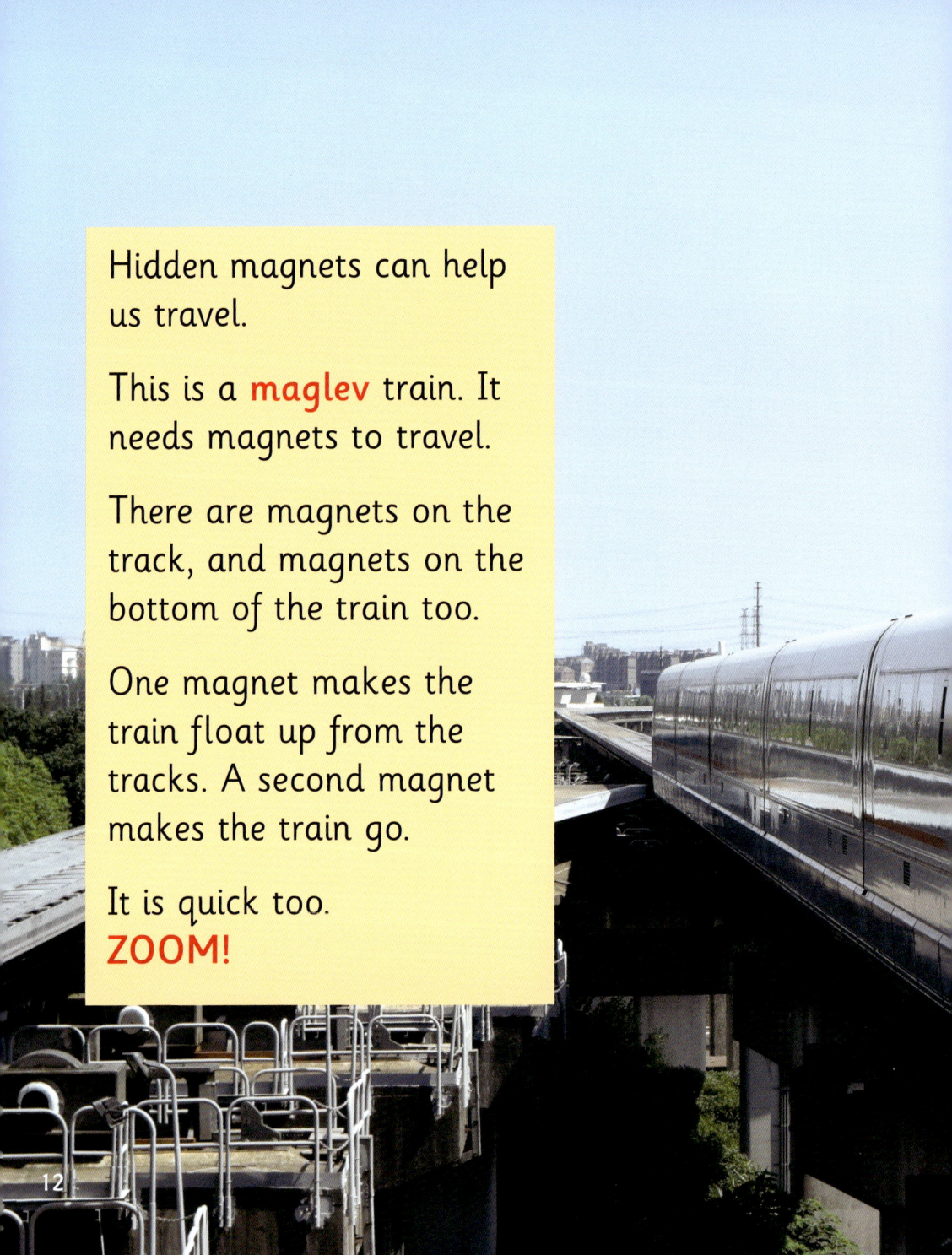

Hidden magnets can help us travel.

This is a **maglev** train. It needs magnets to travel.

There are magnets on the track, and magnets on the bottom of the train too.

One magnet makes the train float up from the tracks. A second magnet makes the train go.

It is quick too.
ZOOM!

Magnets are useful for sorting out metals. This is good if you are in a scrap yard.

Some scrap metal will stick to the magnet and some will not.

Some magnets are so strong that they can lift up a car!

When you go on a magnet hunt, which hidden magnets do you think you will spot first?

Good luck!